Enjoy
Rosfield

S&F

Beyond the Beach

Richard D. Stafford

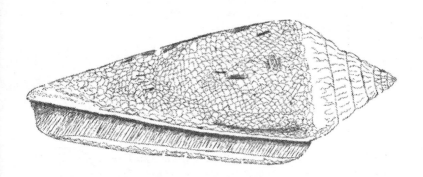

SF COMMUNICATIONS OF GEORGIA, INC.

TEXAS ✴ GEORGIA

SF COMMUNICATIONS OF GEORGIA, INC.
P.O. Box 8
Demorest, Georgia 30535
1-800-357-6301

Copyright © 1999 by SF Communications of Georgia, Inc.
Cover layout by Rosy Donnenwirth
Technical Assistance by Digital Impact Design, Cornelia, Georgia
Screened shell drawings by Patsy Pearce
Shell drawings on chapter title pages by Britton A. Sukys
Edited by Marybeth Wallace
Shell photography by Dick Stafford
Quote on page 12 used by permission from Gulf Publishing Company and taken from *A Field Guide to Shells of the Florida Coast* by Jean Andrews, copyright© 1994.

ISBN 0-9650478-3-0
Stafford, Richard D., 1951
    1. Non-fiction inspirational 2. Men   3. Shells
          I. Title
First Printing, Summer 1999 by Lightning Print,
a subsidiary of Ingram Book Company
Bookstore orders only, call 1-800-937-8000

1 2 3 4 5 6 7 8 9 10

PRINTED AND MANUFACTURED IN THE UNITED STATES

U.S.A. $ 8.95
CAN $ 13.95

For
My Father

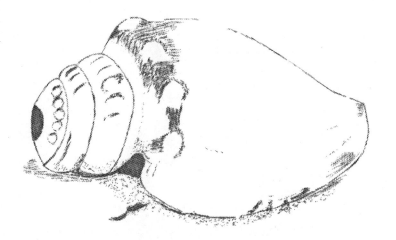

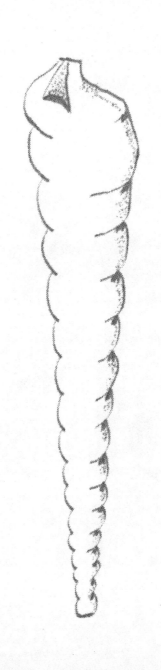

Preface

A beach is a magical place where one can forget the pressures, responsibilities, and frantic pace of daily life. It becomes a playground for young and old, alike. For many of us it holds such special qualities that a visit, however brief, becomes a near-holy experience.

Almost fifty years ago a wonderful non-fiction, inspirational book was published for American readers. This short book centered on the changing role of women in the early fifties by drawing analogies between sea shells found on Captiva Island and the role of womanhood. Even today it is a great book. I have enjoyed reading it many times over. I love the story. I love the Island, too. But I am a man. My shells may be different.

The rustic cabin where much of the above book was written still graciously welcomes guests, but now cars line up at the toll bridge across from Captiva and sometimes it can take hours to maneuver one's way to the Island. The quaint by-ways are abuzz with retail shops, small inns, and restaurants. The roads are now paved. Parking areas are packed on warmer days. Life can get hectic in this paradise. Certainly, it is still a place of great charm and extraordinary beauty, but the Island is no longer what it once was. It is less secluded and more commercial than it was in the early 1950s.

During a recent visit, I longed to recapture the spirit of Captiva's shells, but in a way that might be more meaningful to men. The world has certainly changed for all of us in the last fifty years. As we approach a new millennium, men and women use a different set of rules for understanding their relationships, their responsibilities. The male identity in particular has changed vastly in the last fifty years. Life can be frustrating and disappointing if we fail to understand our roles: how they have changed and how they haven't.

With this thought in mind, I looked for another beach, one that might bring forth new shells. Shells that might tell a different story. To find these and explore their meanings, I traveled up the coast to an island that remains environmentally much as Captiva was five decades ago. I went to Dog Island near Carrabelle, Florida and chartered a small boat for the crossing. There is no bridge. There are no phone lines, no resorts, no paved streets, no retail stores. The island does have electricity — on most days — but I found it inspiring to write only by sun and candlelight.

The shells I discovered are different from those written about so carefully and lovingly half-a-century ago. These shells — the Common Sundial, White Wentletrap, Common Baby's Ear, Angel Wing, Auger, Fighter Conch, and Purple Sea Snail — may provide clues to our identity in this new era. The shells remind me of who I am as a man, a son, a father, a husband, a believer, a fallible human being, a teacher, and finally, an individual with hope. Lastly, they have provided me inspiration as I live, work, and play in today's world.

My spirit has been reawakened by examining this newly found assortment of shells and the meanings they may hold. I hope you'll find a new way of looking at your life within these shells from *Beyond the Beach*.

Beyond the Beach

COMMON SUNDIAL

ANGEL WING

COMMON BABY'S EAR

SCULPTURED TOP SHELL

PURPLE SEA SNAIL

FIGHTER CONCH

WHITE WENTLETRAP

FINE-RIBBED AUGER

GLORY OF THE SEA

THE ISLAND

C O M M O N   S U N D I A L

Torrential thunderstorms precede my arrival on Dog Island. During an eight-hour drive I am pelted with hail and blinded by heavy rain, which, as if planned by some silent force of nature, finally drifts southwest off the coast as I approach Carrabelle. This quaint fishing village is the jumping off point for the Island.

A small boat with a friendly captain ferries me across the bay to a landing where a year-round resident escorts me down an ankle-deep sandy road to a small cabin. I had arranged to rent the tiny beach house on stilts for two weeks. The weather clears and a bright sapphire blue sky greets me as I stand on the small, cozy wood porch.

Gulf waters still churn and crash wildly onto the sun-bleached shoreline as the early summer storm subsides. The eerie drab green ocean is capped by white effervescent surf which explodes up and down the beach and quickly evaporates into nothingness. In front of me, the sound of the water is powerful and strong, constant, like a giant uncontrollable crowd of cheering spectators. But I am alone.

After emptying my backpack and unloading a box of food, I follow the rickety boardwalk to the beach. Rosemary Bush, a dune shrub with short, fine needle-like leaves grows alongside the wood walkway in large clumps. It flavors the cool, crisp air causing my nostrils to flare. I want more of it; to stand there on the boardwalk and gulp it in. The scent of wild Rosemary on a summer beach makes me "inebriate of air," as Emily Dickinson wrote.

As the tide edges out, the sun drifts closer to the western horizon, back-lighting the purple storm clouds out over the Gulf. This thin rim of jagged white light looks like brilliant neon tubing or maybe lightning that has been tamed, frozen in time as a frame for angry clouds now impotent. This stretch of beach is practically deserted. The nearest house is at least half-a-mile farther down toward the deepening sunset. Looking east, I can't see any houses up the coast, and that is good.

Although the waters continue to break with tremendous force against the shore, the ocean slowly retreats. Low tide has begun and, with each succeeding incursion of waves, more and more beach is exposed. The receding water reveals hundreds of sea shells, scattered up and down the beach as if someone had stumbled and spilled a bucket of perfectly selected specimens, leaving them strewn like jewels torn from a broken necklace. Now they wait for a hand — anyone's — to capture them for display in the morning light of a window. My first reaction is to gather as many as I can — as quickly as possible. I am like a child who is making his first visit to a beach. I want every shell. I selfishly want to collect all of them before another beach stroller can snatch them up. And then I realize how ridiculous this impulse is. There aren't any other people on the sparkling stretch of sand. I am the lone beachcomber. The shells lay exposed for me and the morning tide alone to claim. So I relax, overcome my initial greed, and leave most shells on the sand, watching them paint the beach like a colorful Monet canvas. It seems somehow too perfect for reality. There are so many bright shells in such varieties that the shoreline looks surreal. I have never witnessed such a collection offered up by a storm.

At last, my eyes discover an especially interesting shell, coiled, circular, like a bronze medallion left on the sand by an ancient Greek argonaut. In fact, it is a Common Sundial. I pick up the shell and hold it in my hand as the last amber rays of the sun illuminate its form. It is a series of circles, which become smaller and smaller until the smallest surrounds a tiny dot at its nucleus. This Sundial will become my companion for the evening. I have picked it, or has it chosen me to begin my journey?

Once the sun dips beyond the ocean, and the sky turns darker shades of violet and then deep rose, I head back. Along the way, the bright shells that had earlier decorated my path in colorful designs and shapes now become mere darkish spots on the graying beach. Dozens of small sand crabs scuttle out of my path as I near the cabin. The Sundial safe in my hand is ready to tell me stories of ages past and ages yet to come. For sundials are eternal, measuring life second after second, minute after minute, event after event. . .

I eat several pieces of fresh fruit and gaze at the Sundial as it lies on the table in the living area, lit by a nearby solitary candle. Outside it is black, quiet. This candle I have chosen in place of electric light — for simplicity — makes it possible to experience the shades of light and shadow in a more interesting way. After all, those who have observed the moon through a telescope know its surface is more enchanting at those points where darkness meets the light, illuminating the various craters and mountains. The positive and negative light defines its form. At full moon, these details are washed away by the brilliant light reflected off the Earth. Too much light distorts, here and in life generally. A single flame will therefore light my cabin this night. The candle, its reflective glow slightly magnified through a glass hurricane shade, reveals the truth of the room. I can see more in this light. More detail in the shell and more detail in my life.

The shell measures less than two inches in diameter. Its circles contain tiny, rust-colored squares which alternate with a tan background made more golden by the candlelight. The shell looks richer by this light which warms the room with occasional sputters and flickers. It really becomes a medallion, an award for my patience and control of my greed. This one shell projects more beauty than if I had covered the table top with dozens of them. It causes me to think about my life and the trophies I have collected.

My office walls are too full of medallions. A Ph.D. hangs prominently on a wall behind my desk, surrounded by other certificates of educational honors. Each represents yet another rung in the ladder of life and success. These, in turn, are framed by other treasures: teaching awards, community service recognitions, and the like. The wall is a tribute to collecting too many shells, too fast. The individual accomplishments lose meaning when grouped *en masse*. The money, the hours, the investments suggest that I have strolled down the beach of life with a giant bucket pitching in every shell I could find, as fast as I could. Keeping them all, might I have prevented others from enjoying their own opportunities? This feeling leaves me empty, wondering if I am spoiled and greedy. If I desire too much? If I have to have it all?

I am reminded of a young girl in my community who wished to play the piano. Her family decided not to purchase a piano immediately. Once a week though, during her hour-long lesson, she had the opportunity to practice on a piano as she received instruction from her teacher. The rest of the week she had to improvise. She took a long cardboard box, opened it flat, and cut out a section fifty-two inches long and five and one-half inches wide. On this narrow piece of cardboard she painted forty-eight white piano keys, thirty-six black ones. For over a year this teenage girl practiced six days a week using the flimsy cardboard keyboard. Surprisingly, at the end of her first year of lessons and during her recital, over a hundred people watched her play and all agreed she was the most talented student in the class of almost three dozen young people. I am beginning to understand that I don't need all that I have, to accomplish all that I wish.

As the light flickers from the cool breeze, almost going out at one point, I think of my college roommate. We were not mirror images of each other. He was stooped, stiff from disease, and he drooled. Because of an illness, his speech was slurred, his movement clumsy. We met the day my parents helped move my things into the dorm. My side of the room had a new bedspread, matching curtains, rows of pressed shirts and trousers hanging neatly in the closet, a new stereo, an electric typewriter, an over-sized unabridged collegiate dictionary, a pencil holder with dozens of freshly sharpened pencils, a day planner, posters on the wall, all of it. Each of these was neatly in place.

My roommate had only an Army duffel bag and a typewriter, the old klunky manual type. From the worn green bag he pulled a frayed notebook. The binder contained hundreds of sheets of paper which for some time remained a mystery to me. After a few weeks, I asked him about them. He told me it was his poetry. I was shocked. Here was a young man whom almost everyone on campus avoided, often changing directions unobtrusively to escape eye-to-eye contact with him. He had no friends at his dinner table, no late-night collegiate discussions, no dates.

Because he could not hold a pen or pencil in his water swollen hands, the young man typed his original poetry slowly, one finger at a time. Since junior high school, he had been composing these sonnets. Each was an insight into his soul, a window revealing who he was and what he was becoming at age eighteen. One evening he invited me to hear his poetry. We sat on his bed and he read the lines in his garbled diction as I followed along by looking at the words thoughtfully typed on each page. Because he allowed me this opportunity, I discovered my roommate to be one of the most intelligent and sensitive persons I had ever known. His poems were his awards, his trophies, his shells.

My Sundial reminds me of those college days and my roommate. How did I lose what seemed so clear to me during those two years we shared that same small space? In time, he helped me to put away the bedspread and matching curtains. Most of the shirts went into boxes under the bed; only one pencil remained on the desk. He taught me to do with less, to find significance in the insignificant. And then one fall night he left me and the rest of humanity forever. The hundreds of poems soon disappeared — forgotten, as did his lessons of life. Until now.

The days preceding my trip to Dog Island were filled with way too much. The concentric circles on Sundial are a reminder that I need far less than I am consuming. I have horded all the shells that I have stumbled upon in life. I have spent beyond my means. There is far more plastic than paper money in my wallet. I have saved too little, gained too much weight, wasted much, and not cared enough for what is really important in life.

Tonight, my Sundial will help me focus on what is valuable. It will teach me not to pick up every shell I see along the path. Sundial will be my guide, my reminder each day as it spins into each new month and new year. I will treasure the round shell I have found on my first day following the storm. I will take it back home. If I am lucky, the Sundial on my desk will be what is noticed first. The clutter in my space will become secondary. I hope that Sundial will attract the attention of visitors to my office and become the center of our discussions. It will help us to remember to be cautious and selective. Not to horde. To be simple. Sundial will be our focus rather than the multitude of other "shells" filling the walls of my office.

A N G E L   W I N G

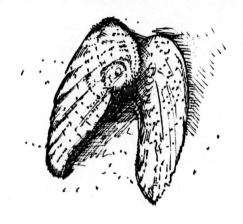

My first morning on Dog Island is a glorious one. The sun is sharp and bright, the wind more calm following the storm, and a pack of gulls fill the air in search of breakfast. I too eat, fruit again, and half a raisin-cinnamon bagel. I wash it down with a glass of cranberry juice and set out to discover the next shell. At the end of the gray splintered boardwalk, almost unseen as it blends inconspicuously with the white sand, the shell greets me: An Angel Wing.

I wasn't really expecting it so soon. Wasn't even looking for a shell, yet, on this morning. I thought I needed to search longer for this one, to carefully weed it out from all the rest. To spend some sweat, blood, perhaps out-right failure before it came to me. But here it is. I didn't even have to step off the weathered walkway. The angel is before me.

The intricately sculptured shell lies flat on the sand, fully open with its outer side facing up to expose its feather-like spread. It does indeed look like angel wings. It appears as if some heavenly visitor had flown over in the night and merely lost her matched pair of wings, which then fell gracefully to this beach. These wings must have belonged to a wonderfully attractive angel. They certainly look so.

I sit on the last step of the boardwalk and reach down to scoop up the wings from the soft sand. They are light, translucent, matched perfectly, and joined by a single hinge. I pull my shell book from a rear pocket and read about this angel:

"Umbones prominent, located near anterior fourth shell: umbones well separated from raised umbonal reflections; protoplax triangular in outline, entirely chitinous, mesoplax calcareous; apophyses large..."

I laugh because I haven't a clue about what any of it means, though I am certain the description is true and correct. But the words are technical, marine biological gibberish and cacophony. I just know that when I look at it, even when I first looked at it, without actually knowing it's name. . .that it was beautiful. It reminds me of my soul mate. My loving partner in life.

Happening upon the Angel Wing is very similar to the first meeting of my wife, as well. I wasn't at all looking so closely for a wife. In fact, I wasn't looking at all. Had even told a close friend that marriage was not in the immediate future. He disagreed. I suppose he saw something that I had not on the beach of life. Perhaps he had his eye fixed on the sand and could see the Angel Wing which had fallen from the sky, just before my footsteps.

She had been recently bruised when we first met. Her longtime sweetheart had walked out, just prior to their engagement, leaving the beautiful twenty-one year old for me to find on a beach after surviving her own storm. She has, for almost twenty years, seemed to be that perfect angel.

I know in order to get this shell back home I must treat it carefully. I must cradle it in opened hands, not smothering or gripping it too tightly. It must have every opportunity to show the world its wonderful concentric ridges and contoured lines which extend the entire length of the shell. Any unplanned or unexpected movement could break the hinge, fracturing it into pieces instead of leaving it whole. She is fragile.

If the Angel Wing is to be displayed at a party, everyone will gather around. They will circle the beautiful shell and listen to her tales. Like the sound of waves wafting from a larger conch or whelk, everyone gathers excitedly to hear each word. They listen to believe, to escape their own problems, to be entertained. They laugh, smile, touch her arms, her hands, hug her neck, and marvel at her lines. She is, after all, the center of attention. Always will be.

Recently, I was to meet the Angel Wing in London, following several months of being apart while we carried out our individual responsibilities. The Angel had been watering a multitude of plants out on the covered porch and heaping great amounts of pet food in various piles for our animals. In her departing excitement, the Angel had locked the balcony door and found herself stranded, fifteen feet in the air. No people nearby. No phone. No key.

Needing to leave for the airport shortly, she crawled over the railing and jumped twice her height into a bed of ferns. In doing so, she twisted her knee badly, to the point she could hardly walk. At the airport she nearly fainted from the pain, but continued toward her destination. No doctor, no hospital. Only a mission to complete.

In London she arrived in tears, caused by the pain

and swelling, as well as fear in how I might react as we started our fourteen day *backpacking* excursion in Scotland, Wales, and England. There was indeed some discomfort on both our parts. We made a change in transportation — a rental car — and soon, the tears became laughter and we ended up having the opportunity to drive around the Isle of Skye, listening to Scottish music, sun roof open, and a magnificent blue sky pouring into the car.

On a train we would have never seen those same emerald green hills, dollops of white sheep, and gentle waves of fog. Blaring Scottish music on a packed rail car would not have been possible. We also found several B&B's, made new friends, discovered many Scottish remedies for a twisted knee, saw old castles, all of which we might have missed had we been on the train. This Angel Wing can turn the worst into the best.

Often, she will change the words of popular songs on the radio to send subliminal messages to those of us in the car. Well, maybe not always subliminal. As if nothing is awry, she sings out these newly created lyrics to familiar songs. To our sons, she changes "My heart will go on, forever," from *The Titanic*, to "You will phone home, tonight." To me, "Do you need to stop for directions?" replacing other original lyrics, "Do you get the sense of my direction?"

As a teacher, this Angel Wing ignites the classroom with clever ideas and surprises. When studying Michelangelo and Renaissance Art, she has students tape paper to the underside of their desks, lie flat on their backs on the floor, and draw upside down. Their arms in the air, they learn patience, commitment, and even the discomfort of painting the Sistine Chapel. All this with Vivaldi's *Four Seasons* softly playing in the background.

She controls the check book with the agility and assuredness of an acrobat. It needs it. If I performed this monthly feat, I would have crashed to the ground like the great Wallenda. I have several times. She knows how to make pennies stretch, steal from Peter to pay Paul, and find money for a night out at the local hamburger restaurant even when it seems the balance line should be zero, or worse.

She is the everything of everythings. She can talk on the phone, roll enchiladas, mop up goo on the tile floor, and read the last lines of a novel. . .all at the same time. Me, I just sit back and marvel. How lucky am I to find this Angel Wing! How could I have survived without her? What would I do if she ever left? I don't ever want to know.

I have my responsibilities, too. And like Captiva, the

world has changed. I cannot sit and watch as she directs the household orchestra. I, too, am involved. I must play my part. It is not just me who is tired at the end of a long day, a long week. We both are. But why should she be the one relegated to the kitchen? The vacuum cleaner? The toilet bowls? School projects? Ironing? Picking-up? Shopping for groceries? Straightening the closets? Washing the windows, the mirrors, the clothes? Our union is a shared adventure.

If I don't know how to do these things, she will teach me. Together, we will teach our sons. They will understand that sexist lines drawn in the sand are soon washed away by the gentle lapping of ocean waters. The beach is shared by everyone, and the responsibility to keep it orderly and functioning, likewise, belongs to all.

I take the Angel Wing back up the boardwalk to the modest house. I place it beside the Sundial. Now, I have rediscovered a better sense of direction and am reminded of my responsibilities. I am also reminded of my extraordinary lover. A partner with whom I will share my collection when I return home. Will she pick the one that represents her?

Happy and not looking for shells now, I return to the peaceful beach for a splash in the aqua water as two dolphins swim by, entertaining me on this deserted island.

COMMON BABY'S EAR

There is no doubt about it — the shell I pick up several days into my stay is an ear. And just as its name proclaims, it even looks like a baby's ear. The shell, a Common Baby's Ear, is found near a group of rough oyster shells, making it easy to spot because of the stark contrast to those around it. It seemed as if that gang of oyster shells were holding the Baby's Ear up for all to see there on the beach. A new gift. A new delivery.

The bleached white shell is smooth and curved, pure and innocent. It does not appear to be spoiled by the life-long adventures of the surrounding oysters. It has not become stained with age spots, wants only to be loved and treasured, is not yet ready to set off on an oceanic voyage. The delicate Common Baby's Ear takes me back to the birth of my two sons: their small bodies hopelessly dependent upon their mother and me for life. They unknowingly look toward us for nurturing care, acceptance, and of course, rewards.

My oldest son now approaches his last days in high school and will soon depart for college. The Baby's Ear causes me to wonder if I have guided him in the right direction. Does he know how to make decisions without me? Does he understand that it is okay to run the vacuum cleaner or clean the toilet bowl, that it doesn't challenge his maleness? Will he get up for class? Will he study? Will he hand in his assignments on time? Will he treat his new friends and teachers with respect and great care? Will he be considerate of the feelings of others? Will he use the correct fork? Will he not fart in public? At least not too loudly. Will he drink himself into oblivion one night in college and up-chuck on his dorm floor? Will he then clean his dorm floor? Will he wash his clothes? Will he avoid all illegal drugs? Will he smile often? Will he occasionally shed a tear? Will he be giving and forgiving? Will he. . .

The Baby's Ear in my hand seems safe, protected from the harsh waves of the real world. Even normal waves — waves that are not part of a storm but ones that can still do damage, even destroy a Baby's Ear — will certainly surround the life of this shell, perhaps all shells. How do I know when to let go? How do I know when to allow the shell to make its own decisions? Fall flat on its face? If I fail to let go, the Baby's Ear will never harden to the rough and tumble world of beach life, never learn what to avoid, and on what to cling. My intellect tells me to set it down and let it experience all that is. But my enormous emotions scream for safeness, wanting nothing more than to provide protection with my fatherly hands. Wisdom from my own bumps-on-the-beach will shield this shell and keep it safe. Alas, I cannot do that. I cannot hold on too long. I know it must survive on its own. I must let it go. As I raise my shell-clad-hand, looking out to the blue Gulf waters, my arm cocks back pointing skyward for the launch, but my throat tightens.

At the last minute the shell goes back into my pocket, not this time, not out to sea, not yet. The texture of my fingers on the soft Baby's Ear in my pocket reminds me of another young person, not one of my own. This one I met on a hiking trail, many miles from the beach, up in the Appalachian Mountains the day after Thanksgiving. Not too long ago.

For most people, this Friday meant meandering

through "mall trails" in search of a perfect gift, a gift that would be long remembered by the recipient. On this, the biggest shopping day of the year, I was on a trail, but not one in a mall. And I did receive an extraordinary gift, simply by being on the right trail at the right time.

The day was wet, but not cold, and the uphill, mile-long trail to the two-hundred foot tall waterfalls was slippery. The rhododendrons were headed off for a long winter's nap, and the lush green ferns were beginning to wilt from a recent and sudden drop in the late fall temperatures. My seventy-three year old mother had asked to see the Falls to take photos of them for her college photography class. What energy she has! The rest of the family was off shopping.

After spending an hour taking dozens of photos, we started back down the narrow and sometimes rocky trail, passing others who were headed up to see nature's beautiful bounty. At a quaint foot bridge, we paused while a group of motorcycle-bikers crossed over, without their bikes of course, laughing and having fun on this holiday weekend. The group, about twenty in all, were dressed in black leather, sported untamed beards, and displayed a variety of silvery metal chains and purplish tattoos.

As the last of the group moved off the wooden bridge, I could see a head bobbing up and down just past the final biker. It was a youthful head and the kid seemed small from my vantage point near a giant hemlock tree growing, strangely enough, out from a massive rock ledge along the trail. The boy moved closer and suddenly I could see more clearly. He was not as young as I had first thought. In fact, he seemed to be about sixteen years old. I mistook his age because the boy had no legs and very little body below his waistline. He was maneuvering the trail by placing his gloveless hands out in front of himself on the rocky surface and swinging his torso up even with them. On this long, uphill trail covered with a thin layer of mist, it was inspiring to watch the boy move higher toward his goal.

As he passed my mother and me — seated on a rock bench — I caught sight of his youthful, angelic face. He seemed startled. I was. So was my mother.

I asked her softly if she had any more film and she said perhaps one shot. I told her I wanted to take his photo and she insisted that I would need to ask his permission.

When I tapped the black-haired boy on the shoulder farther up the trail just before the hemlock tree, he turned as if shocked by my touch.

"Do you mind if I take a photo of you? I mean, what you are doing is just incredible!"

"Incredible? No, this is how I get around everyday. There's nothing incredible about it," he said, wiping dew or sweat from his brow upon his white, sleeveless tee shirt.

"Yes, but on your..."

"Hands? I walk with my hands."

Embarrassed, I felt as if I had intruded.

"Well, yes, it just seems so inspiring," I stumbled out and continued, "It's just that I've seen forty-five Thanksgivings and you have made this one rather special for me. Really!"

The boy turned on his hands and faced me more directly.

"Mister, no one has ever told me that before," the youngster revealed, his adolescent voice breaking from something other than his youthful age, and then I continued.

"You have given me, well, a gift. I don't know you, don't know where you're from, will probably never see you again, but thanks."

"Where do you want to take the picture?" he quizzed, giving in to my admiration.

"Here's fine. With the tree behind us."

So we posed and my mother snapped, a tear clearly visible in her eye as we looked toward the camera. I stood up and told the boy thanks, again.

"Sure, anytime."

Bending back over I got closer to his ear and lowered my voice for only the kid to hear.

"You know, everyone you passed coming up the trail, and everyone you pass when you go back down will get the same feeling from seeing you as I did. You will make this the most memorable Thanksgiving for all the hikers on this trail today. Each will remember seeing you for years to come. They will go home this evening and tell their friends and relatives of what they saw on this trail. You will have given them all a special gift. Hundreds of them. Your presence is an inspiration to all!" I smiled, he cleared his throat.

"No one has ever told me that in all my sixteen years. Do you honestly think so?"

"No doubt. Absolutely, no doubt at all."

We shook hands, he smiled, turned and thrust his calloused hands forward on the rocky path toward the Falls. I watched for a brief moment and then my mother and I crossed the short bridge and turned to the left down the trail. I paused and looked back and there was the boy, looking at us. He was right under the tree which grows from the rock. His hand went high in the air and he flashed us a "thumbs-up" sign. His smile was broad, his face aglow. I was covered with goose-bumps. He had truly touched my soul.

A few days later, upon her return home, my mother called to give me some disappointing news. The photo had not come out. It was gone forever. I was distraught, and then she said something I'll never forget.

"You know, that picture of the boy on the trail is far more clear in your own mind than on photographic paper. It will never fade or become lost. It will always be sharp, clear, and untattered." She's right, of course. But then, she always is.

***

My shoeless feet feel warm against the sandy beach. I stop walking for a moment and remember where the tree grows from a rock, where decades of time have passed as persistent roots of a giant hemlock tree slowly creep to find water and nourishment in the tiniest of crevices and fissures. Even in such a harsh, rocky environment those roots slowly but surely find their way to life. A miracle it is, yes, a gift from a wonderful trail and an equally wonderful youngster. A youngster who found his way, one hand at a time. He has helped me to have faith in my own son's journey through life, a journey which he will soon begin on his own. The time has come to set him free.

I reach back in my pocket, my throat even more tight now, almost choking me. Tears stream down my face as I think of my own sons, the one about to leave, the other still a child searching for direction and discovering more of life each and every day. I think about the boy without legs. Alone on the beach, I cry out for direction, my face soaking wet from my own emotions and the cool yet equally salty mist from the sea. My hand goes to the bottom of my pocket and once again pulls out the pure white Common Baby's Ear. I look out to the blue water and lunge the delicate shell out to the ocean. At last, I have let go. Please find your way, now.

SCULPTURED TOP

I find the Sculptured Top Shell not with my eyes, but with my feet, or more accurately my right foot. I literary step on it, which pierces my foot, making small bloody spots everywhere I walk on the sugar white sand. I am not delighted about my injured foot, but then the shell is indeed an extraordinary surprise.

Finding the Sculptured Top Shell in this manner is not unlike numerous trips into my twelve year old's room. It is almost impossible to enter his carefully guarded territory without stepping on something: electronic games, wood chess pieces which appear to have been blown off the game board by more than just a battle of wits, a dream catcher fallen off the wall, tiny metal cars, other unidentified metal objects — probably characters from some horror movie, a menagerie of his own sea shells collected from previous beach visits, a leaking beanie something-or-other, a two week late and unreturned video that escaped our mad rush to the movie store, a gold Boy Scout neck tie slide, the companion Scout tie secured in at least a dozen merit-badge knots, and an unwrapped but uneaten chocolate kiss that actually resembles a Sculptured Top Shell.

His life is one of many facets. In addition to all of the items above, his attention is grabbed by living things, such as three or four frogs covertly hidden in a cardboard shoe box in the closet — with hopes of hearing indoor croaking in the middle of the night; previously living things such as a jar of fire flies he had intended to let loose before they gasped their last bit of air and flashed their last twinkle of phosphorescent light; and those things hanging somewhere in between: the lost hamster that has nibbled on bits of carpet or petrified oatmeal cookie crumbs for six months and still hanging on to life by only a thread. . .and a scrumptious pencil eraser.

Still he is precious. My son that is; I want to kill the hamster.

I place the top shell in my hand and carefully examine it. The shell looks like a cone-shaped pyramid made perfectly round by the ebb and flow of the water upon the beach and its own genetic mapping. It also looks like a miniature top, just as its name suggests. It almost appears that one could carefully wrap a small string around it, yank hard, and watch as it hopped and bopped, spinning there on the tightly packed wet sand. This shell is different from the others I have found. It spins to its own drum beat, not hearing much more than that which comes from a six inch monitor speaker on the computer game, the voice of a close friend on the telephone, or the latest CD.

At this age, the Sculptured Top Shell is in his own world. Hugs from Dad are not allowed in public, a kiss on the forehead is absolutely out-of-bounds, discussions of girls privy only for his best friend's ear. He eats, sleeps, eats more, does homework only when threatened within an inch of his life or off-time from the computer. Sometimes he communicates more with unseen, unknown hyper-space associates in youthful chat-rooms, than with his own parents. And that's scary.

My own innocent Sculptured Top Shell world of *Leave it to Beaver*, brightly colored, ice-cold aluminum drinking glasses, and balsam-wood rubber-band propelled air planes has given way to people wanting to establish friendships with my kid on the Internet, manufactured plastic tasting hamburgers that seem the same whether they are purchased in Dallas or Denmark, and miniature, remote controlled race cars that can fly down the street faster than my golden retriever can run. If the college-bound voyage of the Common Baby's Ear seemed frightening to me, then I haven't seen anything, yet. The world of my twelve year old Top Shell is filled with condom advertisements in comic books and sporting magazines, vile language in popular music, and middle school classrooms splattered with blood, bullets, and contempt.

I feel the texture of the Sculptured Top Shell with my fingers. The ribbed concentric circles start at its flat base and encircle perfectly until they disappear at the pointed top. The coloring of this continuous line, too, seems perfect, though I am not asking for a perfect child, or a perfect world. I know I have made mistakes along the way. He has, too. But to relinquish my young child — not even officially in his "teens" yet — to the harshness of the beach would be irresponsible. I cannot sit by and allow him to wander about in the current age, removed from our father/son relationship. As his father, I have a responsibility to know whom he is talking to on the web. The food he eats must be safe and nourishing. Not imitation everything. It is I, his parent, who must listen and understand what the music is saying when he clicks on the portable CD player. We must talk about it, even when connecting to the music seems impossible to me. I will not hand off these responsibilities to others simply because I am too busy, too tired, too old.

It is important to know that I am not a prude. I will enjoy wine along with a loaf of sourdough bread later this evening while sitting out on the small deck. If there was a beach party or ball game on the tube (no TV here, though) I'd have a beer. Though I don't smoke, I may even puff on a cigar tonight. I am willing to openly and frankly discuss sex. I will even tell him an off-color joke when the time is right. But I am not willing to hand him over at this stage, a mere toy top spinning haplessly through adolescence, to strangers or an unsafe environment. I am his father, and I will do my best to protect and teach him. That is the charge for all fathers, no matter our marriage status, our profession, our skin color, our income, our pastimes, our own distractions, our everything. We must do our best to protect and teach the youngsters we have brought into the world. We must not run away. No matter what.

Recently, shortly before Father's Day, I was returning from an out-of-town trip in the car. On the radio I heard a report which stated that half the kids in the United States are from single parent families, or at least from other non-traditional families. The same report said that in most major cities, within certain neighborhoods, over seventy percent of children are without their natural father on Father's Day. Our beach is full of banged-up Sculptured Tops, wanting nothing more than a string and kind hands to give them direction and momentum.

It becomes the problem of all who walk upon the beach to help lost and meandering shells. If we do this, if we help them to find a purpose in life, it may prevent their being covered by millions of grains of sand, buried by the weight of our post modern culture, or whatever current sociological term is in vogue. They will not sink below the surface and be recruited by the lowest level of sub-culture to the electronic-moronic age, only to become twenty-first century trash, a by-product of monetary greed, selfishness of time, and a burnt-out-over-spent society.

The fathers of our beach must return to be fathers. They cannot be like the loggerhead turtle who deposits its eggs and then swims off happily to life-ever-after to some other island. Fathers who are no longer part of the family must be encouraged to fulfill their commitments. They must provide the resources to raise the Sculptured

Tops, provide time for play with them, and offer emotional support and guidance. Our society requires more instruction and licensing for the driving of cars than instruction on how to be a good and responsible father. The laws of the beach may need to be changed to encourage some fathers to understand how important their role should be. More helpful, though, would be a change in our general cultural attitude, instead of more laws. If we are *expected* by society to be responsible, then a change in fatherly behavior becomes far more likely than if forced by legislation.

When I return home I will talk with my young son. I will ask him to play basketball. I will challenge him to one of those computer games that fascinate him so much. I'll listen as he pops in a CD. Who knows, I may even reach back into the top shelf of the kitchen cabinet and fill up a couple of those dusty glasses — those colored aluminum glasses from my own youth — for us to sit and talk about frogs, fireflies and tops. It is after all my responsibility to teach and protect the Sculptured Top Shell I have found.

PURPLE SEA SNAIL

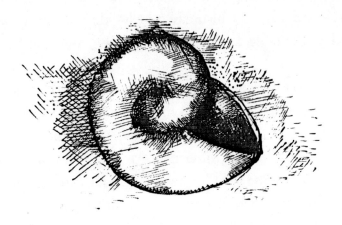

My parents have finally retired. Only recently my seventy-four year old father turned the key to the front door of his real estate office for the final time. I watched as my mother emptied the last of his office trash cans. Old real estate and insurance forms, discarded photo copies, faded faxes — all once urgent bits of information needed for concluding a big sale — even a stained Styrofoam coffee cup has now been swallowed up by the last of the giant black trash can liners. The red twist-ties at the top of the bags bound together these final remnants of their thirty year old business: a business which sent their children to college, paid for cars and houses, erased hospital bills, answered the phones, brought the latest technology in home sales to customers, helped fund the U.S. government, provided a few vacations at the beach, purchased years of birthday and holiday presents, put food on the table, kept the lights burning, and so-on and so-on.

Still, outwardly, they are in good health. But those days will draw to a close in the future. One at a time, I have seen my grandparents pass away, then older aunts and uncles. Today, these two are post-war survivors. They work in the yard for hours on end: cleaning, tilling, planting, weeding, pruning, harvesting. . .all for the future. They never stop. Never.

They are the Baby Boomers' parents. They had little when they started their families after the great War. They went to college for free. They tried not to get into debt, but when they did, they paid their bills on time. They didn't lie. They went to church. They both worked. Hard. They seldom took vacations. They slowly graduated into bigger homes with more bedrooms, but only when they could afford them. They never heard of braces. They did not own a charge card for many decades. They only knew one kind of mustard. Their telephones were always attached to the wall by a cord, unless someone got mad, which seldom happened. They never rode in a limo. They bought lots of groceries with saturated fat. He never cried. She never complained.

Surprisingly, after many decades of marriage they are no longer married. Surprised? They are still friends, though. Thankfully. They visit. Talk. Drink coffee. Plan their separate days. They show compassion and care for the other when each is ill. But now, they no longer share the same roof. At times, I wonder how this could have happened. I don't know. I do care, though.

Amidst all the yard work they do in separate yards, each always rebuffs me for being too rushed, too over-worked. They always announce upon my arrival, without fail, "You're working too hard. Driving too much. Flying too much. You need to slow down your pace. Sit down and relax." I do sit down for a moment and look back up at each of them standing there before me, their mouths awry from fatigue. Sweat rolls from each of their faces, off their chins, and into the earth. Garden dirt sits comfortably under their nails, exhaustion fills their breath. *I* need to slow down? Doesn't either of them own a mirror?

With this recent memory in mind, I sit on the beach before the waves, smile, and realize how these two indi-viduals are like the the Purple Sea Snail I have just dis-covered hiding under a piece of gray drift wood. The snail shell is empty, its former inhabitant gone elsewhere. I pull a small magnifying glass from my pocket and examine the shell more closely. Its opening is wide, even wider than the bulk of the shell itself. Its overall size is small, but its opening is giant. No door, only openness to the world.

The purple shell seems to beckon all to enter. It is a friendly shell. Its texture is without lines, ribs, or bumpiness. It is smooth and defined more by color and its inviting entry than by anything else. It is fragile, but survives because of its ability to float in open, warm waters. It seldom sees the bottom of the ocean floor, but rather enjoys life nearer the surface, out at sea, always moving. It is a traveler — a doer — driven by the ocean current and its own desire to go places. It is free, but also safely cradled by the ocean herself. It is the ocean that propels and keeps the Purple Sea Snail alive, escaping a deadly crush if it descended to the floor. The ocean and the shell work together — each complementing the other — and the result is a shell that survives for all of us to enjoy. To learn. To gaze upon. To marvel.

These are my parents, indeed many post-war parents. They have traveled a great distance to arrive at this point in their lives. He was a War hero, flying for four years inside a giant bomber in the South Pacific darkness, only eighteen years old. A faded black and white photo shows this young kid standing under the fuselage of his B-29, three of the four propellers shot to pieces on a final mission. Countless heroic medals lie hidden in the back space of his top dresser drawer. He *never* talks about them. Men from his generation simply don't.

My mother is all fun. She played football in the yard with us years ago, staged practical jokes, and has a constant smile on her face. With little college education she rose to the level of business loan officer of a large bank by being both savvy and kind. At age seventy-four, she is taking a final college course to earn a degree in what else, but horticulture.

These two are always in motion. Not just physically, but mentally as well. They surrounded their family with years of warmth, like ocean waters ballasting the Purple Sea Snail high on the open sea. Our home, like the entrance of the shell, was always open. The house was a hotel during our youth. Four boys, each four years apart, provided a constant flow of youthful friends and guests into our home for almost thirty years — from the first Boomers, to the last.

They are like the color purple of this shell, as well. I will always remember them as being like royalty. Not stiff and formal royalty, but special like a courageous and beautiful king and queen. They are purple in every way, even today.

How can I provide the same kind of openness and royalty for my own children? How can I imitate the patience and play they gave the four of us? If there is one mark I have missed which seems so important, it is play. It seems that to be good parents we must remember to play with our children. We must forget we are adults — parents — and play like a child alongside them. It does something special. It frees us from all the garbage we have collected over the years. Recently, while raking leaves in my mother's front yard, she told me to come quickly and see what was in the giant pile of red and yellow fall leaves where she sat. Almost fifty years old, I rushed to the leaves expecting to find a snake, or some bizarre insect. I bent over curiously, and my gray-haired mother — screamed — and threw a mass of colorful leaves into the air, laughing out loud. She knows how to play.

If we only find the time — or make the time — to play with our kids, we will discover what freedom it brings. A beach is a great place for that chemistry to happen. Digging holes in the sand. Making a castle. Running in the surf. Diving for treasures. Yes, playing with the shells, making funny faces in the sand with them frees your spirit, awakens your soul, calms your life.

I will never forget the patience my father taught me as a youngster. During my first year at college he was kind enough, perhaps naive enough, to provide me with a new, sporty red car. The car got tremendous gas mileage and was perfect for long trips between school and home. Unfortunately, the new car did not have a radio, or even an eight track tape player, which was a necessity for an eighteen year old in the early seventies: great car, no music.

The day before I left for school, Dad suggested we install an eight track player in the dash board instead of under it, as most people did at the time. Right off, I could see this was a good idea. It was a small car and a dangling tape player would, no doubt, bang the knees of front seat passengers. So we began looking for the right spot in the dashboard.

As it turned out the only place was the glove box which was equipped with a foot-and-a-half black plastic door that swung down when unlatched. Dad opened and shut the door several times. And then, as if a light bulb had suddenly been charged with electricity, he announced,

"We'll remove the glove box door and mount the eight track directly in the dash!"

"Hey, good idea Dad, but how, I mean, if we remove the door?" He explained that we would make a wood replica of the plastic door, cut out a rectangular hole for the player, and then mount both back in the dash. Presto! A classy car with sound. Dads are so cool.

"Let's do it!" I urged, only to Dad's calming and practical observation.

"Oh, we can't do it today; this will take some time. Patience. It's going to be a while."

"How long, Dad? Can we do it by Sunday?"

"Well, a few weeks, at least," he answered assuredly.

With that, we took off the glove box door and he began making a pattern out of paper, slowly, making sure the drawing matched exactly the black plastic door. We reinstalled the small door and it was time to pack and leave for school. Off I went, a three hour drive, Dad back home plotting and planning the new wood dashboard.

Several weeks later I called and said I'd be home Friday afternoon. Dad said he'd been hard at work on the project and that he couldn't wait to share his work with me. When I got home he had placed on the dining room table a piece of redwood, cut exactly to the shape of the glove box opening. It looked just like the door in size, but was still rough on the edges and both sides.

"Dad, it's not finished!"

"No, but it's on the way. Before going any further, we have to make sure it will fit. Time spent sanding and finishing would be wasted if it doesn't fit," he taught me.

So we took the wood piece out to the car, removed the plastic door, and placed the new wood panel in the dash.

"Perfect fit!" I exclaimed excitedly.

"Well, almost, but this corner, over here on the bottom right, needs to be curved just a bit more."

"Dad?!"

"Patience, son."

We took the board into the small shop and carefully trimmed the lower corner of the redwood panel. Slowly and meticulously we reshaped the wood until, upon another fitting, the board matched exactly the opening in the dash.

"Let's cut the hole for the player. Want to?"

"What about the edges? We need to sand the edges. And the front surface, as well," Dad instructed.

He handed me a sheet of sand paper and I sanded. And sanded. And sanded. Until Sunday afternoon, I sanded.

"Let's cut the hole, Dad," I suggested.

"Not yet. We need to buy a tape player," he announced. And so we did.

After careful measurements, Dad had me draw a rectangle on the wood surface. Then he pronounced the drawing to be exact, and instructed,

"Getting late, time you hit the road, isn't it?"

I said only one word, which he lipped in mime, "Patience."

About Halloween, I headed back home, expecting to install the great wood dash board and tape player I had been telling all my friends about at school. At home my father said he had a surprise. He brought out the wood board. It was indeed nice. He had crafted the hole and continued sanding until the piece of redwood was like smooth glass.

"Let's put it together."

"Well, we want to make sure it fits, the board, the tape player, the whole thing."

It did.

"Now, we have to install three, or maybe four, long screws out the back, probably countersink them in the front side, in order to actually mount it. We'll need a brace in the back to support the player, too."

"Well let's go," I said, ready for the project to end, so the music could begin.

We went to the hardware store and found long, skinny screws, and a bracket, and went to work. I had planned to go out with my old high school friends so Dad stayed up late and worked on our project. Sunday, it looked almost finished.

"What about the surface," I asked, knowing it wasn't going in the car this weekend again.

"Do you think natural redwood color would be fine?" he quizzed.

"Sure."

I retuned to school, and called home a few weeks later, near Thanksgiving break.

"How's it going, Dad?" Not expecting a conclusive type answer.

"I believe you'll be happy," he said, in a fatherly voice exuding patience, thoughtfulness, and kindness.

Wednesday, before the holiday, I arrived home and he had finished. He showed me the fine, smooth wood dash panel, cut to hold the eight track player which was still in the box. The glossy surface showed off the wood grain and had a deep red color. It was slick. And on one side, just to the left of the tape player opening were white, old English letters, "RDS," my initials.

I shook Dad's hand and he smiled. We mounted the new wood dashboard and wired the eight track tape player. We got in the car, I drove, and we listened to the new tape I had bought, "American Pie." What an afternoon it was, a shiny wood dashboard, a father's smile, and finally, my happy ears.

Four or five years later the car was demolished in a bad accident. I was not hurt seriously, and in a few days my dad took me to the wrecking yard where the car had been placed. I took a pair of pliers and a screwdriver with me. All the way there my father kept saying that saving the tape player wasn't important. Not at all. We'd get another with the insurance money. He was the agent, after all. Once at the car, I crawled across the front passenger seat and unfastened the wood dashboard and tape player. The eight-track fell away to the floor as the entire wood piece came loose from the dashboard and into my hands.

"Good, this is what I wanted," I announced, holding the board and smiling. My father put his arm around me and we headed home. That was over twenty-five years ago and now the redwood board sits on a bookshelf in my office as a reminder of the gift of patience my father gave me. In turn, I hope to pass along the treasured gift of patience to my own children.

***

The Purple Sea Snail in my hand reminds me of all that my parents were, all that they are now, and all that I hope to be. They are royal and smooth and open to the

world. If in the end, their own health fails ever-so-slow-
ly and they don't pass away quickly from this world, it
will be my responsibility to keep them in my home. Here
they will live. It is my charge to care for them. To hold
them close no matter what dreadful disease attacks their
bodies. To keep them happy. To keep them safe. To play
with them, even when they painfully fail to recognize my
own face staring back at them. This I know I will do.

Finally, with the shell in my hand, I sit thinking about
the ocean and my parents. How there seems to be a par-
allel between the two. Why do we come to the beach?
Perhaps it is because we love it, and even fear it. The
ocean is a place to love because we can play, let go,
become children again. It comforts us like a parent does.
After all, we call her, "Mother Ocean." We love the surprises at the beach. The imagination of sculptured
images in the sand. The cool water against the hot sun.
The secret of what it hides. The gifts found, scattered
there on the beach.

But there is an element of fear, as well. We know the
ocean can bring forth tremendous storms, causing
destruction and pain. We know that mystery lies below.
We can't always see the confusion and turmoil which surrounds life under the glassy surface. Sharks, hungry
crabs, jelly fish, sting rays and the like, even tsunami

waves cause fear in us at times. Just as during childhood, at times we fear our parents. We know that at any moment they can whack us on the rear, have us sit in the corner, withhold the car keys, ground us for life. But we understand that there is a relationship between these two things, love and fear. And so we find ourselves at the beach again and again. The ocean is like our parents whom we should always respect, enjoy, and love.

I place the delicate purple shell in my pocket and walk along as powdery sand squashes up between my toes. I wish that my own children were here with me, to dig a giant hole in the sand, to throw a frisbee, to form funny faces with a variety of found shells on the beach. Just to play.

FIGHTER CONCH

This shell is very different from all the others I have collected. The rest are almost perfect examples of their various species. They are as many shell collecting books define, "Gems: perfect examples of an adult shell." This shell is less than perfect. It does not rise to a Gem, or even a Fine or Good. In most shell books, and to most shell collectors, it would be classified only a "Poor." But that's okay.

The short pointed spines which normally jut out from around its crown have been worn almost completely away. Only bleached white dots remain. In fact, the very tip of its crown is missing. Its color, once a brilliant red-

dish brown is more mottled and frosted now. The door,
or operculum area, is rough and ragged. It is an old, tired
shell that has seen better beaches. But in spite of all this,
it is still in some ways a very handsome shell.

The Fighter Conch gets its name because it is indeed
a fighter. Expert shell collectors will tell you that an
inhabitant of one of these three-inch shells can leave a
whelp on a hand just by the force of its slapping operculum. When a collector reaches for a live Fighter Conch,
the animal quickly turns over to defend itself with great
zeal. It may be frightened and bruised, but it does not
give up easily.

At times I feel a lot like a Fighter Conch. While I
have faced only a tiny handful of tragedies in my life, the
everyday bump and grind, ebb and flow, have at times
left me feeling more like one of these small Conchs than
the famous Glory of the Sea shell you will read about
later in this reflection. Life can do that to a person.

Some years ago, just after my thirtieth birthday, I had
the devastating experience of ending another person's
life. The man was a highway construction worker. He
was merely doing his job in a dangerous situation. There
was little warning for the traffic that approached the
work zone, and no one in the particular area was flagging
motorists or warning workers of possible dangers. In the

blink of an eye my automobile tossed the man to the ground, leaving his wife a widow and his five children fatherless.

I cannot begin to tell of the guilt, the frustrations I felt then and still carry today in relation to this horrible event. I am seldom on the road where the accident occurred, but when I am, the man's face turns to me on the side of the road and stares back at me. It is as if he were shouting a last minute plea, "What are you doing? Steer away! Steer away!"

His is a face that will never disappear from my memory. Not ever. The reminder of it has worn down the spikes of my Fighter Conch. The color of this shell has faded from the reminder of the loss his family suffered. The edges of the door have been made jagged and life isn't so smooth at times. How do we survive after this? How dare I even think about my *own* survival?

But survive we must. It must have something to do with the understanding that life is a lot like most shells. When you hunt shells on the beach only a few seem perfect, to be a Gem. Most are chipped, or broken, or faded, or otherwise eroded by constant rolling in the surf. Imperfection is the rule, not the exception. Both for shells and for people, too.

Life is full of events that can erode one's shell. These

events range from losing a job, to broken relationships, or to fighting a deadly disease like cancer or AIDS. Steady disappointments can cause serious illnesses: high blood pressure, heart disease, mental illness, gastrointestinal problems, strokes, obesity, accidents, and as we have seen, even death. The havoc played upon our shells can be devastating. But the important thing to remember is that they *can be*, not necessarily *will be* devastating.

What we have to do in life is to become a Fighter Conch. We cannot lie down and be steamrolled into oblivion by the crashing waves of despair. There is, after all, nothing I can do to bring back the man whose life I ended. Not hope. Not money. Not even prayer. None of these will cause him to reappear and once again become part of his family in flesh and blood. His body is gone. Only memories remain.

I must first accept the reality of what happened — no matter how disastrous — and then put on my armor. I must hold strong against the erosion caused by guilt. The cracks caused by fear. The faded glory caused by self pity. I must ask for forgiveness, seek peace, and find meaning in what is left. I must go on. To lie down and be tossed about by the salty foam will only destroy me. I must be responsible and get on with my life. I cannot look backward for direction, for it is in front of me. I cannot sleep in the past, but must finally awake, and arise alive.

Just recently I received word that a former student, one of the most talented students whom I ever taught, ended his life. How frustrating it was to hear this sad news: how he must have felt like a Fighter Conch that had given up to the oceans of despair. Why couldn't I have been there? How is it that no one was there in those final moments — those dark hours of fading light — to take his hand and show him the real spirit of the Fighter Conch? How could it have happened? How could it have been avoided?

I am convinced now, more than ever before, that we must be strong. We must all be like the Fighter Conch. We must ride the surf, but not give in to it. We must enjoy the sun, but not be burnt to a crisp by it. We must drink the cool waters, but not drown in them. We must warm ourselves in the sand, but not be buried. We must take in all that life offers. But we must never give up. Never.

My Fighter Conch is not perfect. It is bumped and bruised. But it is here to help me focus on what is to come, not what has passed. It is here to steer me to safety and joyful times in the ocean of my life. Perhaps most of all, it is here to help me see beyond the beach.

WHITE WENTLETRAP

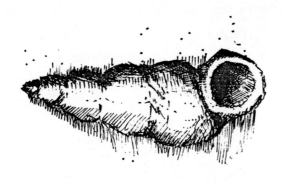

On my fifth day at Dog Island I am greeted with a shell gift. It sits atop the gray post at the end of the boardwalk. It did not get there by accident. The wind didn't bring it mysteriously to my attention. I am not sure exactly how it arrived, but I know it wasn't by chance. Perhaps it was left by the kind lady who showed me to the beach house on the first day. I had told her I was writing about shells. This one, though, is a rare find on the Gulf. Not impossible to find, but rare. To find it here on the post was certainly planned by someone. It is a White Wentletrap.

Wentletraps are miniature, gloriously ornamental,

curved, and solid white sea shells. Tiny cord-like beads encompass the entire length of the shell, rolling over increasingly smaller whorls. The opening at the base of the Wentletrap is perfectly round, like a porthole. It is beautiful. To me, it seems to convey a religious meaning. Its very look is religious and praiseworthy. It appears as if it should be displayed in a place of great honor. Perhaps a holy place.

Not too long ago I had the opportunity to travel to India for an extended period of time. India is full of Hindu temples. The Hindi practice the world's oldest continuous religion. Animals are the center of their lives, their temples. There are large temples in the giant cities of Bombay and Calcutta. In rural areas there are small roadside temples the size of a suitcase. All of these temples contain the offerings of Hindu worship: fruit, candles, holy water, shells.

I never saw a White Wentletrap in India, but it certainly belongs there. If it were much larger (most Wentletraps are only an inch long) it would be the perfect shell for dipping holy water out of a thousand-year-old rock basin and into the hand of a grateful worshiper. The shell looks holy with its intricate design. The white color asserts its purity. Massive replicas of the Wentletrap would fit appropriately on the lower spirals of the greatest cathedrals, synagogues, and temples of the world. There is a heavenly look about this shell.

The shell reminds me of a person I met just a few years ago. This woman had returned to live in our community — her childhood home — after thirty years of absence. She moved away, had been married and divorced twice, had three children. Over the years, both of her former husbands died from tragic illnesses.

She is a teacher, a kind and gentle friend. I met her at a church event the day she returned. She felt led back to the community for some reason, but was somewhat depressed about how her life had turned out at this point. Her family had once owned a large home out in the country, but it had been sold many years before. She had not visited our community in over a decade.

Not too long ago, she drove out to that old house and made a fascinating discovery. Her former family homestead was now a center for locally abused women and children. She was speechless at the revelation. Here was the home in which she spent her entire youth, now secretly housing women and children who had suffered failures and heartache, if not physical abuse as well.

One day she went into the house and introduced herself. In time, she hopes to become a volunteer and help counsel women in the very house in which she grew up.

This friend looks forward to the day when she can say to the women there, "You, too, can leave this house and find a new life. Just as I did." My friend has now found a reason to have great hope. And she is sharing her new found hope with others. It seems to me that the spirit of religion should be centered on this very thing.

In India, my van was often approached by hordes of young people, particularly in the rural areas where they seldom had seen a non-Indian. While stopped in a small town and drinking a cola on a hot and dusty afternoon in the van, I was approached by a large group of boys who stood outside my window and asked if I had any pens. Ball point pens are valuable to the poor of India as it provides them an opportunity to write. If they have any money at all it will be spent on food and shelter, not pens. Told of this before I left the United States, my companions and I had brought along several hundred ball point pens to give away.

As the youngsters stood below the tall van window, I began passing out the pens. Hands of at least twenty youth went into the air grappling for one of the plastic treasures. These boys began shoving and grasping for the gifts. Even as most received their pen, additional hands came from nowhere. Finally, below the long, outreached arms there appeared a small girl. Her short arm extended upward, as well, but only half the distance as her fellow male friends. But her hand was not empty. It wasn't being thrust in my face to receive a gift of a plastic pen. Instead, her hand held a shiny red apple. She was almost trampled by the mob as she tried to *give* me a gift. I leaned out the window, reached my hand way down to hers and took the apple. In its place, without the others seeing, I slipped some Indian paper currency into her hand. It was enough to buy her and her family many meals. She smiled and was surprised. She had been rewarded — many times greater — in response to her humble gift of an apple.

How have our churches learned this simple lesson? Most do all right. Thank God. Some, we have seen in the last few years, have become entangled in getting rather than receiving. A basket full of television evangelists have never learned this lesson at all. Even today, following the folly of earlier TV gospelizers, we find people hawking religion as if it were the next item on a shoppers network show. These people say and do things that Christ specifically mentioned to avoid doing in public because it might offend others.

How often do we use our own religious membership to gain business/personal loans, meet the right people in the community, or finalize business dealings? I once heard of a community which would only hire new teachers if they belonged to a particular church in that small town. How sad.

Many churches — small congregations and national organizations as well — have become havens for gigantic physical life centers, holders of massive amounts of rental and commercial properties, and parlayers of political rhetoric. Membership in some churches is informally dictated by whom you voted for in the last governmental election. In some communities the holdings of local libraries are dictated — not by the majority — but by one or two fanatic religious individuals who successfully obtain the attention of the local media. What has happened here?

It seems that genuine religion and closeness to God is like light. So many of the world's religions use light as a metaphor for the Divinity. Not too long ago I was in a small car heading into a tunnel bored through the side of a rocky cliff in Norway. My wife was driving. My mother-in-law sat in the front passenger seat of the two-door car. I was seated in the back. The two lane road through the tunnel was narrow and long, several miles in length. A rocky wall beside each lane provided no room to move off the road if a problem occurred. Near the deepest part of this man-made rock tube our car came to a sudden and complete stop. The battery and generator had given out. There was no light in the tunnel and nowhere to pull aside. In total darkness the three of us climbed out of the car which sat square in the middle of the single lane. I told my wife and mother-in-law to feel around the front of the car and put their hands on the rock wall. They began to walk away from the car, lightly dragging their hands against the rough surface of the wall, hoping to emerge from the end of the tunnel, which was nowhere in sight.

I went the opposite direction, toward where we had first entered the mountain. I, too, could see nothing. It was absolute black. No flashlight. No torch as they would say in Europe. I was fearful that a car, bus, or truck might come flying into the tunnel and plow right into us, or even worse for another driver, into the stalled car. No vehicles came, though. In time, a small dot of light could be seen. The light sparked a sense of relief within me. A feeling of anticipation. A hope that disaster might be avoided. I continued toward the speck of light more quickly. Faster and faster I walked hoping to make it to the arched opening before another vehicle entered the long black abyss. Finally, I reached the opening just as a long line of cars, buses, and trucks had exited a nearby ferry on one of Norway's most beautiful fjords. I was able to warn motorists of the stalled car, and soon a wrecker arrived to pull the car out, away from danger. Through it all, it was light I had hoped for. Light to provide a sense of direction. Light to show me the way. Light to save my life and the life of others in the blackness. Light had given life!

Sometimes, we find ourselves in our own man-made tunnels surrounded by a void of blackness. Events that should provide light, but instead enshroud us in darkness are perplexing. Even today, we find groups who wish to make prayer legal in public schools and school-related events. In spite of very good intentions, they badger politicians, find their own slate of candidates who support their views, and run down anyone or anything that gets in the way. Whose prayer do they want? Christian prayer? Well, I am a Christian and I do pray. I absolutely believe prayer can change lives. Remove guilt. Allow forgiveness. Heal. Express joy. Unify. Provide direction. Open hearts. Reduce greed. Bring acceptance. Demonstrate love. Show the way to peace. All of these. But there are other religions and religious denominations in our democracy. If our government — congress, the courts, or a constitutional amendment — provided for recited prayers in public schools, certainly it would not be for any *one* religion. Not even Christianity. Some think otherwise.

Our country is a democracy and if structured prayer were routine in public schools, surely the courts would agree that prayer by *any* religious group would be acceptable. That means along with Christian prayers — Hindu, Muslim, Jewish, Buddhist, satanic. . .all religious groups would have an opportunity for recited prayer in public schools. Would we pray to Mary the Mother of Jesus? Allah, the Father of Islam? Buddha, the Eastern God? The Hebrew God, Yahweh? Ganesh, the elephant God of Hindi? Jesus, the Christian Son of God? All of them seem valid. Or would we as a nation, simply agree to level the praying field and pray to just plain God? Most can see the trouble this change would cause. Those who can't see end up frustrated.

For many, it is crucial to possess religious convictions and values. For most, life is neither full nor rich without belief in something greater than ourselves. But we should be greatly concerned when a few in any one group — religious or secular — attempt to dictate the religious thoughts, morals, feelings, and desires of all of us.

The Wentletrap, in all its splendor and glory, has become misused. Religion has become the political muscle in congress, in courts, in communities. I am not sure that when I look at the Wentletrap that this is the direction that churches should take, no matter what their faith or religious doctrines might be. Seems most world religions believe in some fairly common ideas: be kind and caring toward your fellow persons; don't steal or hurt; forgive; share; praise your deity; and love others as yourself. Seems simple enough. Why use the purity of the Wentletrap to influence narrow and self-serving moral beliefs for those other than ourselves?

I will be leaving the Island in a few days. I have left the Wentletrap on the post at the entrance of the beach as a public (even if I am the only public here) symbol for the purity and individuality of world religion. Allow all their own space to believe as they wish. The ornate shell marks the Temple of the Beach clearly. Others can stand out there on the road, if they must, and shout their selfish moral desires for the world to hear. But don't disgrace and defile the purity and perfection of the Wentletrap and the beautiful beach where it lives.

The mission seems simple enough:

Treat others with kindness. Forgive and forget. Live and let live. Hold all life sacred. Find something good to say about everyone we meet, even those everyones who turn out to be people we cannot stand. Share all we can; push greed away. And most of all, search for the Light of

Understanding. A Light that will show us the way. A Light that reflects the purity, gracefulness, and perfection of the Wentletrap.

CHAPTER EIGHT

FINE-RIBBED AUGER

Near the end of my stay, I sit in perfectly clear water just a few feet from shore. My hand digs in the fluid sand. Surprise. I find an Auger. But not one. A whole colony. Within a minute I am holding a dozen Augers, each about an inch in length, gray and tan in color. The Augers are shaped like ice-cream cones. Then more Augers. Suddenly I am holding an entire handful. It's a group, increasing in numbers, still. Like the way a school classroom grows during the first few days of the academic year. I wonder when it will stop?

Teaching has been a part of my professional life for many years. I have seen switches turned on, faces light up, the answer suddenly discovered, the world opening its doors. It is an exciting place to be every day. The process is the same whether one is teaching kindergartners or college students. Thankfully, the reward is the same, too. Those who have been selected to be teachers know this feeling well. It is what feeds us. What motivates us to keep going. It enlightens us. It is our own switch. Our own light bulb. It is worth far more to us than the check we receive at the end of the month.

The Auger is so much like a growing mind it is uncanny. The shells move in packs. They stay together, for security, for survival. They depend upon each other. They grow together. Augers are determined, too. In rough seas they bury themselves safely in the sand, until the storm has passed. Protected.

Oh yes, one end of the Auger is pointed, sharply. It can, and does, make its point. Inappropriately. Appropriately. And it can hurt either way. Augers are often painfully blunt. They know no other way.

The Auger is seldom alone. When one finds an Auger alone, there is usually a reason. A reason that needs exploring. It could be hurt. Scared. Mixed-up. There may not be anyone around, in his part of the sea, to show him the way. Often, it is our responsibility as teachers to help an Auger find its way back to the pack. If it fails to do so, it may not survive. Or at least not survive as well as it could, should.

I recall a graduating senior who needed only a "C" in my class to graduate. He had a poor record in both grades and behavior. In the week preceding his gradua- tion, the Auger realized he had not completed many assignments. His average was much below a "C." He was disgusted as he leaned over my desk, looking at the reality there in the grade book. In anger he put a finger to one of his nostrils and blew hard; the content of his nose spewed across my arm. I just sat. It was perhaps the most challenging — even disgusting — moment I had faced in teaching. The Auger ran from the class.

I sent word to the shell that he could make up the work, but that it must be completed before the end of the week, before graduation. Magically, all the missing work appeared in my box, in his own handwriting, and I gave the go ahead for his graduation.

Years passed and I was on vacation — six hours from the school where I had taught — in an ice-cream shop with my twelve-year-old son. We were eating ice-cream cones and in strolls the Auger. He looks at me and then continues to the counter. Suddenly, he realizes that his former teacher is there in the shop with him. The lone Auger gets his cone and turns for the door. But he stops short. He stops at our table and speaks.

"Could I talk to you for a minute?"

"Yes, sit down."

"I, uh, want to apologize for how I acted before I graduated. It was all my fault. I am sorry. Will you forgive me?"

"Of course. I forgave you the day you completed the assignments and graduated."

"I want you to know, I am about to graduate from college. I have one year left. I am planning to be — and I know you are really going to be surprised about this — a teacher!"

"Well, yes, I am surprised. I am proud of you. Good luck," I responded, as the Auger smiled and left, licking his cone.

He had found his way; he had joined the group. And I am sure that if he is successful in his career as a teacher, he will have his own "Augers" to help, to direct, to forgive.

Over the years, many of my students have gone on to become teachers. I have had the opportunity to observe many as they seek their teaching certificates. It has been exciting to guide and steer them, observe them in front of the class, experiencing victories in the development of their teaching skills. What joy it has been to see these

Augers help turn on the switches, light up the faces, discover the answers, and open the doors of the world for many other Augers.

G L O R Y   O F   T H E   S E A

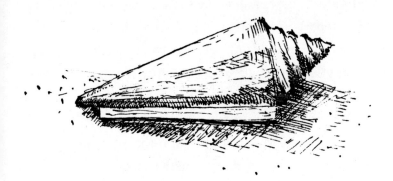

This shell, Glory of the Sea, was *not* found at the Island. In fact, other than the photograph, I have never seen one. The only reason I know of its existence is from a shell book I have been reading along the way. The shell captured my eye because of its beauty, which is reflected in its name, Glory of the Sea.

In the past, these shells have had tremendous value. For centuries, they have been considered the greatest finds in sea shell collecting — world-wide. Only those diving in the southwest Pacific are lucky enough to obtain one naturally. The shell lives deep within the ocean, seldom finding its way to shore. Just one excellent specimen can sell for over several thousand dollars. It is indeed rare. It is beautiful.

What causes a Glory of the Sea shell to be a highly sought after possession is the same thing that makes diamonds, pearls, platinum, and gold valuable. It's rare. Unusual. Hard to find. And perhaps most important, not everybody has had an opportunity to experience one.

I have strolled down the beach toward the east end early this morning — the last full day of my visit. Along the way, I have passed a little inn, the only business on the island. There are seven guest rooms. It is a quaint place to stay. No phones, no television, no hordes of guests screaming for cheeseburgers and margaritas while perched, chest deep in water, at a swim-up bar. I assume the few guests I spot on a long wood porch have chosen to stay at the Inn for similar reasons for which I have come to the Island. It is rare. Unusual. Hard to find.

No one comes here by mistake. They don't get lost on the highway over on the mainland and then say, "Where am I?" One comes here with a mission in mind. Or maybe no mission in mind. Or maybe just to clear missions from one's mind, to redefine them, to evaluate them. Maybe to change them. I think this process must be true for many beach visits that people make. But here, on this particular island, the process seems cleaner. Purer.

Sharply focused. Even magical, like accidentally finding a Glory of the Sea shell as a gift.

Indeed, what is rare in life is what is often sought after. If peace and quiet are rare, people seek solitude. If hustle and bustle is rare, people seek crowds. If bananas are hard to find, people will go to great lengths, stand in long lines, pay exorbitant amounts of money just to peel and enjoy one. The list goes on: front-row tickets to a sporting or music event, a new car model, diets, the latest doll, computer and communication technology on the cutting edge, new furniture designs, clothes, athletic shoes, the just released CD, the latest sandwich craze at the fast food, the smallest cell phone, a new hair style, or just hair, period. People often want what they don't have.

What is missing from our culture? What is it that people want, but can't find? What is considered valuable? Rare? Unusual? Hard to find? What is our Glory of the Sea?

I spend all morning on the east end. I pass an Osprey nest sitting precariously on top of an old, twisted pine tree. Hunched on a nearby dune I wonder if one of the white-headed, hawk-like birds still calls the nest home. Very still, I wait. How special it would be to see one of these birds. I've heard their wing spread can be up to six feet. They dive into the water, feet first, to catch their meal, usually a small whiting or mullet. They are indeed rare.

Disappointed, I leave the dune without spotting an Osprey. I remove several leaves off the stem of a Bay Cedar bush by pulling the twig through my fingers. I twist the batch of elongated green leaves releasing the sweet smell of cedar into the air. The fragrance lingers on my hands for a while. It is nature's island perfume.

I walk along the water, ankle deep. Two sting rays just a few steps in front of me rest quietly on the sandy bottom in less than a foot of water. The water is remarkably clear. They sense my movement and scurry off quickly to deeper, safer territory, their long tails whipping the sand as they zoom away.

Several hundred yards out in the ocean a shrimp boat chugs by. Hundreds of gulls follow along the net-enshrouded boat. Further back several dolphins join the oceanic parade. Below the surface, out of sight, I am sure thousands of fish have joined, also. The water is still this morning. It has been very calm the last two days. The stillness has allowed the sediment normally stirred by the ebb and flow of the tides and encouraged by the wind, to sift to the ocean floor. Even standing in water chest high, I can clearly see my feet. I swim and think about this wonderful place I will soon be leaving. What it has meant to me. How it has changed my thinking.

Tomorrow, I will return to the newspapers, TV, cars, everyday life. I will watch the latest "gotcha" story from the "gotcha media." The stories seem to never end. The media's fascination with overanalyzing, over-covering, over-exposing the short comings of all humanity is a part of daily life. The process, we sadly understand, is really a money machine. At times our culture seems like a snake in the dark. It sees something move, lashes out, sinking its deadly fangs, injecting poison. Then morning comes and the snake is surprised that it has bitten itself. Its own tail had seemed to be the enemy, and now it lies dying of poison from its own self-inflicting jaws. How unfortunate it seems for our culture. We dwell on such petty things, holding everyone accountable for everything. It is indeed The Gotcha Society.

Ours is the age of insane accountability; we are afraid to brush against another human being in an elevator or office, or afraid of lawsuits, afraid of not being fair, afraid that someone is going to cross the line we've drawn in the sand, afraid the market is going to crash, afraid someone else's child is going to be selected for something special and ours isn't, afraid the rules haven't been followed, afraid we're going to be hurt or worse — murdered, afraid someone may beat us to that parking spot, afraid we may fail, afraid the lottery will end before we strike it rich, afraid of what lurks in our food — our water, afraid of road rage, afraid, afraid, afraid. . .

The electronic age has solved many problems. It has helped medical care to reach new heights in making sick people well, enabling older people to live longer. It has helped us reach the moon and beyond. It has educated people in rural areas through distance learning centers. It has connected us in ways never before thinkable. Students from several cultures, spread across the planet can meet and visit through sight and sound, learning about and understanding each other in remarkable ways — all electronically. It has helped us to fight wars. To avoid future possible wars. To spy on others. To see from outer space whether people pick their noses or not.

Most of these things are good. Sometimes it becomes misguided, though. What can I do to bring the sanity of my little Island to the insanity of everyday life? How can I keep my spirit focused on the simple, and help those around me to accomplish the same? How do I develop the patience to wait and expect the best out of others before jumping down their throats when a mistake has been made — intentional or otherwise? How can I become excited about what happens to my neighbor in the same manner I get excited about the possibility of seeing an Osprey? How do I make the quality of everyday life seem rare, unusual, and hard to find?

It must begin within. I must examine where I am and what I am made of. I must look at how I respond to the minute-by-minute events that each day brings. I must work to simplify. To look for the best in others. To be intrigued with the unknown. Surprised by the encounters with those I meet each day. I must take time to reflect, to be alone, to be thankful for the little girl who holds the apple out to me. I must revere the people who have passed before me and who may more fully understand the waters I forge, watching for danger, adhering to the channel markings. But perhaps most of all, I need to be more like the people I met in India. People who see their culture interconnected in ways that few cultures on our planet understand. Wanting — even *thirsting* — to learn five different languages, understanding how my responsibility interplays with yours, providing help unasked, and expecting absolutely nothing in return are worthy goals for living a quality life. Being reverent with life and holding all life remarkably high seems to be the key to happiness for those who practice the world's oldest religion. We should do the same.

I pass the Osprey nest on the way back to the cabin and am surprised to see two giant birds diving into the water a hundred feet from shore. They catch fish in their massive claws and fly to the crown-like nest high in the twisted old pine tree. They disappear into the nest, only an occasional wing popping out for me to see. My presence never appears to cause them any concern. We seem to be friends.

As I begin to pack my things this night in candlelight, I think of the parting greeting I learned in India. The word is *Namastay*. This word is spoken to others as you leave and means much more than our "good-bye" or "see ya later." The word is affectionately spoken, hands together briefly as we might do in prayer, and then each person repeats the word. *Namastay*. Simply enough, it means, "In my heart, I wish for you only the best this day. May God bless you!"

In the morning I take my backpack along with the empty box and trash and set them outside the door. For a moment I walk to the end of the wood board walk, the bridge to all I have been given these two weeks, and face the blue-green water that has refreshed my soul, rekindled my faith. My hands together, the word *Namastay* slips from my mouth.

THE ISLAND

St. George Sound

N

The ferry ride across the bay takes about forty-five minutes. The Captain is friendly, less than a dozen passengers visit quietly. Those on board seem to realize what they have left behind. It's much slower than the charter boat I took at my arrival. I hold a drawing of the Island in my hand. It's a simple map. On this paper, the Island looks like a sea horse, maybe a giant sled. A sled that took me to unbelievable places, giving me unbelievable gifts.

There are six young people on the boat — all college students — who had stayed at the Inn on the Island the same time I had been there. They laugh and visit about their plans for the summer. One of them reminds me of my oldest son who will join the ranks of freshmen in some other college this year. They are full of life, happy, and outwardly friendly. I wonder if during their stay on the Island we had shared any similar thoughts. Did they find life there simple? Did they see the sting rays? The dolphins? The Osprey? Smell the Rosemary? Bay Cedar? Were they bringing back gifts from the sea? Could they see beyond the beach? Oh, I wanted to ask.

The Island appears to be growing smaller now as we approach the mainland. Its seven-mile length seems to be a mere hundred yards. Its thick pine forests seem short on the flat horizon, which separates ocean blue from sky blue. The smell of Rosemary is left behind for another visitor. The dolphins on the oceanside are out of sight. The Osprey. . .

As trivial and horribly clichèd as it sounds, "Departing is such sweet sorrow," seems fitting and descriptive of my feelings. A friend recently told me about a visit with her father. The visit took place during the last five days of his life. He was in a hospital and she had been called to be with him from out of town. The two had for many years a shallow father/daughter relationship. During this time he had missed many events in his grandchildren's lives. There was little or no emotional connection between them. He had suffered from depression a long time. Then he became terminally ill. In those last days they each offered unconditional love for the other. Forgiveness soothed the pain, softened the anger, erased the years of disappointments. She recently told me that those last five days of togetherness probably saved her many years of counseling. How fortunate that both were able to find common ground before the end. But how do we push that back? How do we have that conversation years earlier? A generation earlier? How do we offer unconditional love for those in our lives and then wrap those feelings securely in forgiveness, kindness, and honor? How do we visit the Island _sooner_ in life and take what we have learned beyond the beach?

The beach has helped me see the way. It will help me to reach out. Pull in. To extend my care for others in all that I think, say, and do. It will begin tomorrow.

I am excited to drive back home to my family; to kiss the Angel Wing, attempt to hug the Sculptured Top, look the Common Baby's Ear in his eyes knowing the days of his youth in my house are changing like a wind-blown sand dune. I can't wait to see them. To touch them. To tell them of my adventures. To tell them how much I love them. To show them the Sundial. The Wentletrap. The family of Augers. How neat it would be to find a Glory of the Sea shell. How I will search for it daily, hundreds of miles from any beach. Any island.

The drive north is long and dark. I am filled with anticipation in returning home from my experience. The long stretch of highway reminds me of my return home following another ocean visit, just a few years ago. I had led a dozen college students on an excursion in the Bahamas. We sailed a seventy-foot sail boat from Miami to Bimini, Chub Cay, and Grand Harbour Cay in the Berry Islands. On our return home, crossing the Gulf Stream late at night, we encountered a vicious storm. The weather was so violent we lowered the sails and used only the diesel engine. One student remained with me at the wheel; the others were below praying.

The port holes leaked badly, finally causing the engine to quit. In turn, the generator failed and we lost our lights and radio. In the dead of night and with lightning cracking all around, we had to raise the massive sails in order to keep from capsizing in the waves. If you sit, you drown. It seemed that all hope was lost. We were very frightened, all of us. But, at least we were moving. The wood bow of the old boat split the angry waves before us. Suddenly, a brilliant light burst across the beryl-green water, ending the darkness.

My first thought was that an ocean liner was coming

straight at us, the light was so bright. Soon, though, we discovered it to be the U.S. Coast Guard. The lack of lights, sails up in a maddening storm, and no radio response alerted their concerns. They boarded the boat and after some discussion, offered to stay near us until our arrival in Miami. Several hours later, as an extraordinary sunrise greeted us, the South Beach shoreline appeared on the horizon. We thanked the Guard with applause and vigorous hand waving with all on deck. The journey was long, enlightening, and filled with mixed emotions near the end, but, alas we had returned home safely.

❈ ❈ ❈

I understand now, more fully than ever before, how important it is to share patience with my children, those in my house as well as those in my classroom. I know I must find time to play with my kids, even when they are no longer kids. I must constantly help in taking care of the daily responsibilities. To do things even when they don't seem manly. To love my beautiful wife with all my heart. To honor my parents each and every day. I must look within my self, my life, my soul, and find — yes keep — what is simple. Eliminate what isn't, if possible. To follow the Light. As Thoreau taught us in *Walden*, "I want to live deep and suck out all the marrow of life. . .to drive life into a corner, and reduce it to its lowest terms."

Finally, each day, I will look beyond the beach and even though I may not utter it aloud, I will greet all I meet with *Namastay*. Good-bye dear Island.

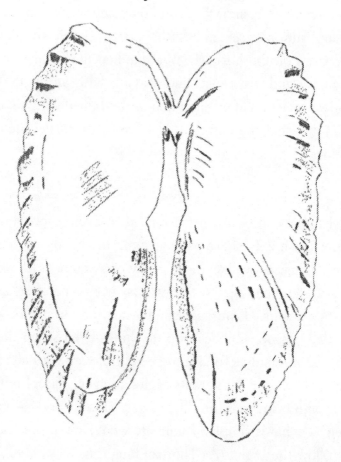

ACKNOWLEDGEMENTS

William Clark of The Vines Agency, editor Marybeth Wallace, Charlie King of Lightning Print, a division of Ingram Book Company, arborist Ed Regan, Jeanni's Journeys and Sue Van Yorx, Suzi Stanton's Low Tide, designer Rosy Donnenwirth, Don Bagwell and Bill Stratton of Digital Impact Design, artists Patsy Pearce and Britton Sukys, Jane Doerfer, owner of Pelican Inn at Dog Island, Rotary International and Jim Kent, Bennett's Fishing Fool Charter, Raymond William's Ruby D Ferry Service, Rev. Janice Melbourne Chalaron, Van Wunderlich and student, and manuscript readers: Willard Pearce, Doris Stafford, Jim and Marge Stafford, Mike Fitsko, Vida Jo and John Wooten, Richard Smith, S.A. Allen, Keith Griggs, Kristal, Daniel, and Kirk Stafford, Dr. Gary Stough, Michael Burnett, Jan Zarr, and Curtis Bradford. Also, thank you Daniel and Tim and my summer school students at Clemson University for their encouragement to refine many of these stories for inclusion in this book.

Also, thanks to Patricia Pope, Frances Peabody McKay and Chris Kelly and Great Outdoors Publishing Company.

ABOUT THE AUTHOR

Richard D. Stafford is a college professor and writer living in rural Georgia and North Carolina. He was selected in 1998 for a Fulbright Teaching position to Asia and has received the Sears Foundation Teaching Excellence and Campus Leadership Award. His novel *The Funeral Club* was nominated for a Townsend Award, considered Georgia's highest literary award. His other works include: a novel, *Summer at Hope's Croft: A Bread and Breakfast Tale*; a play, *Shades of Grey*; "The Thanksgiving Tree," an article published in various U.S. newspapers; and interviews with playwrights Arthur Miller, Edward Albee, Lee Blessing and *New York Times* editor Frank Rich, published in several academic journals. His books are often featured in special events sponsored by the South Carolina Center for the Book in Columbia, South Carolina. He is currently finishing a new southern novel, *Iron Horse*, to be published in summer 2000. He and his family enjoy traveling, sports, theatre, and cookouts with family and friends.